AF322633

本书惠承乐俊民严赛虹基金会赞助出版

乐俊民严赛虹基金会文学 · 人文丛书

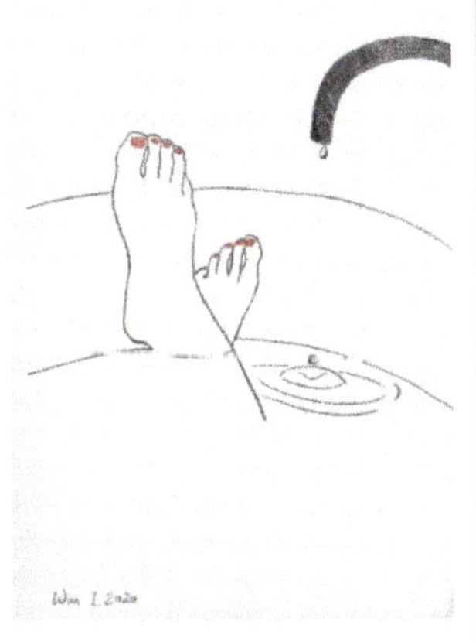

当日子变得稳定焦虑琐碎，放下眼前的生活，去未知的世界游荡。

不惑之旅

左拉

2019 年夏天的日记

九十二天旅行的
散文诗与画

易文出版社 · 纽约

Published by I Wing Press, New York
iwingpress@gmail.com

Journey to Passion

Zora Wan

www. zorawanart.com

December 2022, First Edition, First Printing
ISBN： 979-8-3493-6366-5

不惑之旅 2019 年夏天的日记

左拉 著

责任编辑： 思　渊
艺术插画： 左　拉
美编设计： 王昌华

出版： 易文出版社·纽约
版次： 2022 年 12 月第一版，第一次印刷
字数： 10 千字
定价： $19.95 美元

前　言

"自己，是人需要解开的最终谜团。"美国歌手小萨米·戴维斯曾这样说。这句话像乌云中的一道光，描述了我不停寻找的人生旅程。

我自幼喜欢画画。在上海市艺术学校上过三年的国画和素描。本以为自己会走上与艺术和设计有关的行业，却阴差阳错地进入了会计师事务所。来美国以后，在硅谷的热潮中做财务分析：在几个初创和上市科技公司做到了高管。但总有一种动力促使我去寻找更独特的渠道，道出自己的心声。于是，我师从旧金山湾区的两位艺术家玛西·惠勒和莱瑞·罗宾逊学习油画。他们所鼓励的创造的自由和联想，给予了我继续探索自身艺术表达的更多工具和勇气。

用诗和画配合的形式从事创作，基于 2009 年的一次觉醒。那是来美国近五年的时候，我突然陷入一种抑郁和疏离，感觉外面的世界离自己很远。冥冥中我在一家书店里偶然拿起了德国作家埃克哈特·托利的《新世界：灵性的觉醒》，突然像经历了电击，从自己沉睡的身体中醒来：世界与我的联系变得无比亲切和深刻；时间和空间成为爱可以克服的人为分割。一个精神的空间向我打开。我因此创作了自己最大的一幅红白黑作品：宽四英尺长八英尺、用丙烯塑料为媒体的《生活与爱：超越时空 》（本书封面图）。这也触发了我想用更接近生活的语言，即质朴的诗和红白黑插画，把这种无与伦比的感受，传递给更多的人。

这本诗画集的创作源于 2018 年我与先生的一次承诺：在一次久违的假期中，在圣汤玛斯海湾的阳台上，于职场和生活中都深感疲惫的我们，下了决心，无论先生是否成功地申请到转行的学位，我们都需要一个长假。

因此，这是一个关于放松的诗画集，也是我在那次觉醒之后，在外力推推搡搡又十年后，鼓起勇气停下来，再次寻找自己的诗画集。残雪说过，"人的内心的确有一个深不可测的湖。" 我希望这本书，能带你去体会一场九十二天的修行：在十个国家和地区的世俗体验中，一次释放焦虑和压力的深度放松；一次探索自己内部和外部未知世界并听到心声的旅程；一个把内心逐渐干涸的精神之湖装满的过程。

命运在暗处写着它的指引。将心敞开的时候便能听得到它的喃喃细语。感谢这一路上遇到的引路人和老师：史钟麒、张意、严力和邱辛晔，你们提供的种种机遇和灵感促成了这本诗画集的创作与出版。感谢 Ying

Chang Compestine，你源源不断日臻完美的新作品给予我
启迪。感谢我的知己和好友黄赤子、严珍、Angela Xu 和
Jean Lin，在这段特别旅程中的陪伴。更感激我在上海和
美国的家人们无尽的支持，特别是我的先生 Kevin
Hummel，你的智慧和温柔让我在寻找自己的路上走得坚
实。

左拉 于加州圣拉蒙

目 录

第十五篇：圣地亚哥的奶奶　　/ 72

第十六篇：回家　　/ 76

第一篇：出发

工作是一把石磨
日复一日地把黄豆倒进去
流出来我们赖以生存的豆浆

生活像理发店的地板
每天会有新的碎头发落地
唯有不停歇地打扫才落得清静

就这样磨了数十年
就这样扫了数十年
不知不觉
走到了人生的中间

两颗疲惫的心
两双还能看见火花的眼睛
看看周围的人们啊
满脸写着同样的神情

就这样吧
给自己放一个长假

带着箱子
带着孩子
我们去旅行
没有目的

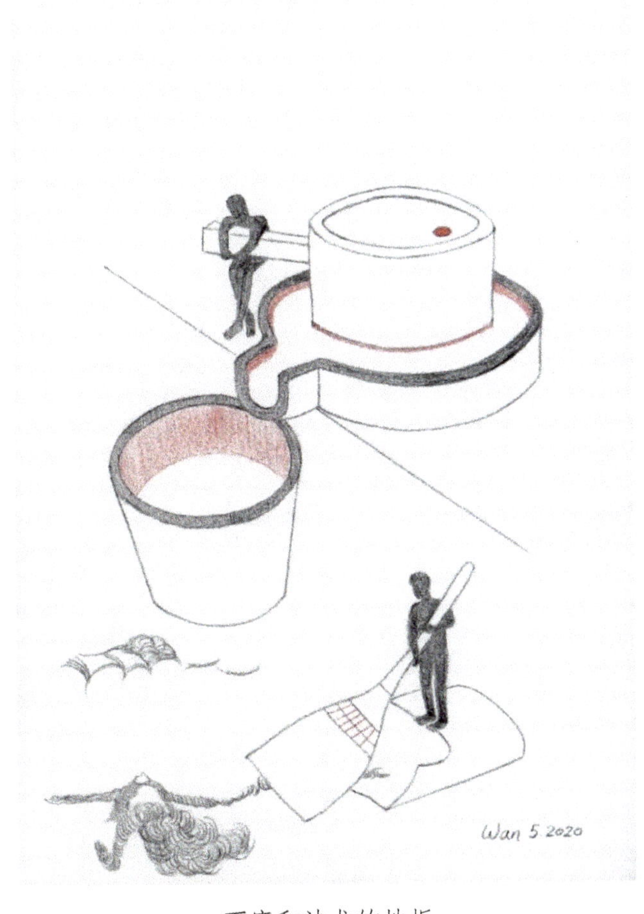

石磨和沙龙的地板

一　惯性

加勒比的可可豆融化着芝士
让热带的能量流动于舌尖
着了火的天空落在大海上
变成了紫色和橘黄
五百年的城墙依然眺望着远方
让看海的目光落在了历史的苍茫

沐浴在这五彩缤纷之下
为何依然麻木紧张
把负重完全放下
为何依然感觉着沉甸甸的份量？

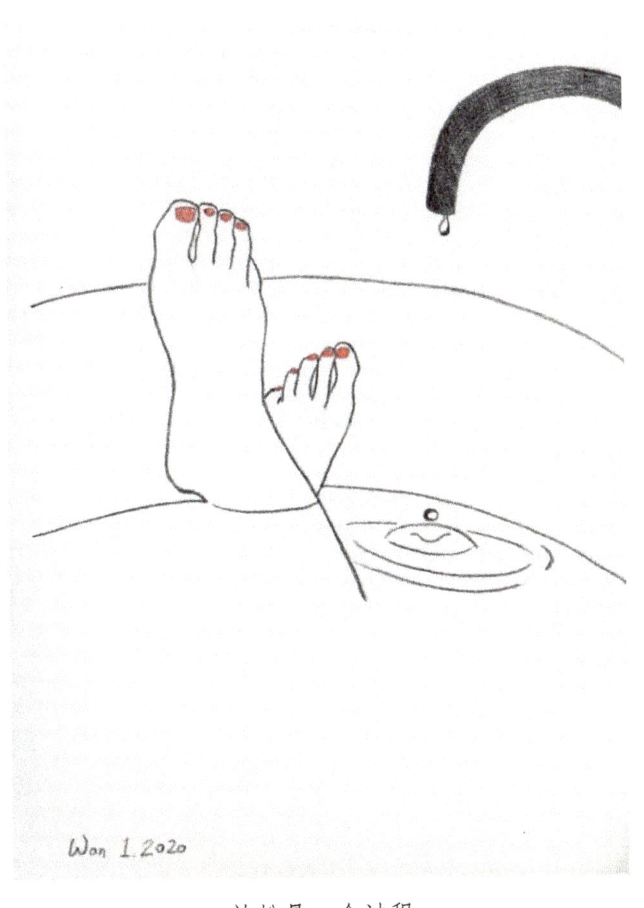

放松是一个过程

二　波多黎各的无言之言

波多黎各人会讲一种无需语言的语言
空气中，赤橙红绿，如音乐般蔓延把人链接

租的车有一个凹陷
刚对先生喃喃几句
一个在旁收拾白衣蓝裤的男人就走来
点点头向里面的白衣蓝裤招手

黑脸的酒店服务生咧开一道白色的弯月牙
摇摇手门口不能停车
我指了指睡觉的孩子
又指了指大堂的方向
他转头就领来了有钥匙的先生

咖啡色的长发如海浪般起伏
几个眼神的流转她莞尔一笑
先租着试试吧
因为买的不是房子
买的是生活方式

言语之外的理解[1]
在这片土地上自然得像呼吸空气
不知何时
我已经将她遗落
不知在何方

1　"If I can understand this language without words, I can understand the whole world."- Paulo Coelho；译文："如果我能理解这没有文字的语言，我就能理解整个世界。"保罗·柯艾略。

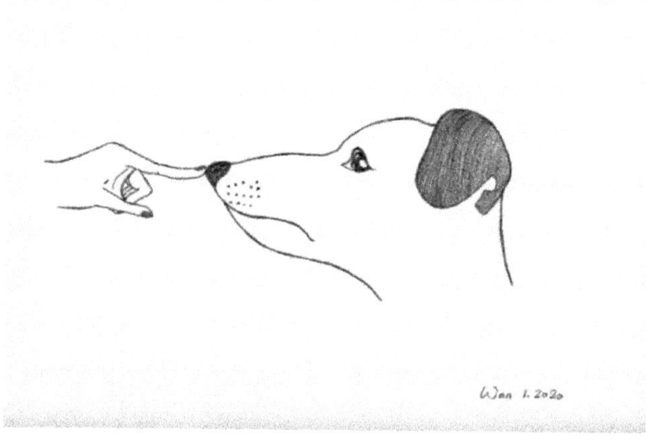

无需语言的语言

第三篇：　魔法圣塔菲

一　　魔法圣塔菲

红色的土
蓝色的天
机场大巴上的女声说欢迎来到魔法之州
一个在太阳下光着屁股没有植被的城市
一个继承着土著红色土坯房的城市
一个有峡谷街上美丽的画廊的城市
一个和 Georgia O'Keeffe 爱与被爱的城市
再次到来
依然新鲜
鲜艳的色彩
干燥的空气
火热的太阳
偶尔来一阵冰雹

教堂里的螺旋梯
像一串 DNA
完美旋转

却受不起生命之轻
可载满人的照片见证了奇迹

一个小小的红土坯教堂里2
十字架前
一个有着红色粉末的土坑
我们各自捧起一撮
在身上脸上涂抹
基督在上
土著在下
这神奇的土能给你带来治愈的希望

Meow Wolf
粉红的巨人
细嗅蔷薇
一个梦交织的存在
我们在潜意识的迷宫里游荡
像极了我们无察觉的生活

圣塔菲
从过去到现在皆沉浸于传奇
阴差阳错又来到这里
仿佛这是我们的朝圣地

2　El Santuario de Chimayo 一个建于印第安人圣地的教堂。

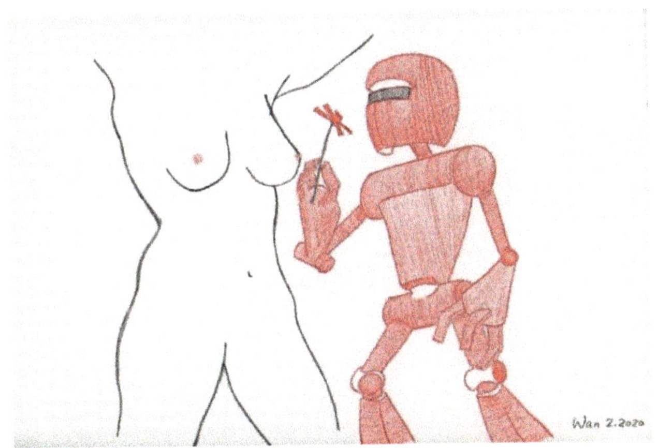

乔治亚•欧姬芙和喵狼(Meow Wolf)

二　圣塔菲的国家公园[3]

一圈埋在地下的地基
一个已经迁徙的文明
九百年前两千个印第安纳人
在这已经看不见的多层圆形社区里共栖息

每天两小时打猎
种种蔬菜和土豆
回来一起讲故事
一个圆形地下室
通风良好
他们就在这里一起向神祈福

妈妈问这样健康生活
他们是不是很长寿？
我想并不是
我们忘了分娩的风险
我们忘了严寒的冬天和炎炎的夏天
我们忘了生病带来的危险

3　佩科斯国家历史公园（Pecos National Historic Park）和班德
利尔国家纪念区（Bandelier National Monument）

我们忘了野兽的威胁
但尽管如此
当他们围着火炉边讲故事的时候是不是眼睛
闪闪发光
当他们一起唱歌跳舞向神灵祈祷的时候
是不是内心充满力量

但尽管如此
我们这些孤独的现代人
为什么想起来他们的日子会有些向往

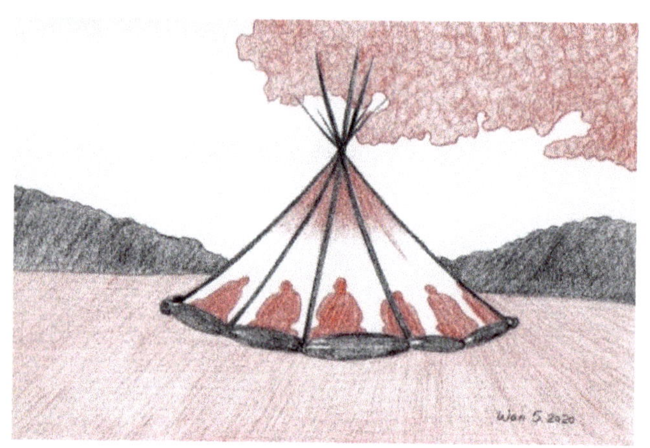

像土著一般地生活和祈祷

三　格兰德河峡大桥

(Rio Grande Gorge Bridge, Taos, NM)

那些纵身跃下峡谷的人啊
是什么样的黑暗抓住了你
一圈红色的鹅卵石包围着一个名字的缩写
我能看到那些被留下哭泣的人们
他们要面对破碎的身体
以及一次次残酷的回忆

只愿你的灵魂像羽毛一样轻柔
在这不情愿的世界里
高高地飘起
让那些爱你的人
记得那绒毛般的温柔
就如生命的开始
母亲的子宫里
那如羽毛一样轻轻的一划

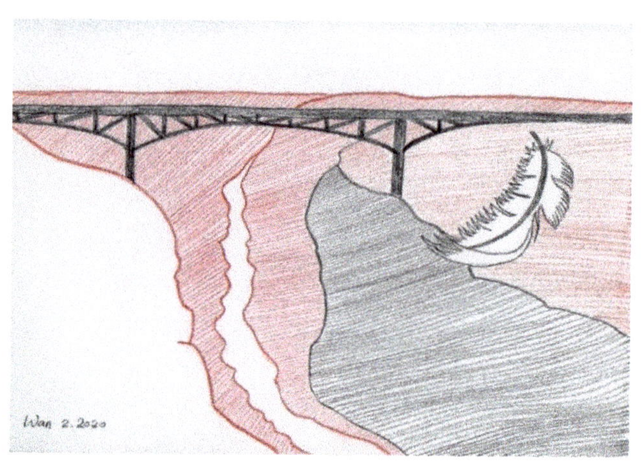

格兰德河峡峡谷上飘扬起的柔软羽毛

一　哥斯特里格的相见

热带的岛屿像一个乐观的绿毛龟
在海里飘着
在它长满绿色丛林的背上
我寻找着心底的未知
借热带的阳光
温润那有点冷却的心

走出冷飕飕的房间
我充满期待地看着
她长卷发修饰的背影
四年不见
她就这样跋涉千里
在这陌生的阳台上转过身

你好
你好
岁月，在笑意充盈的空气中泯灭

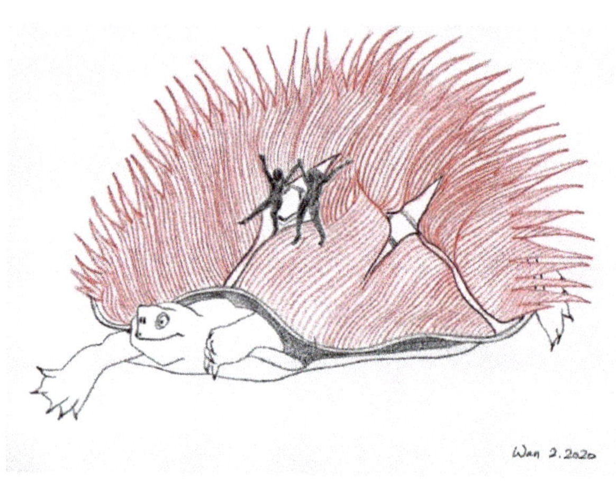

哥斯特里格的岛像只长满水草的乌龟

二　哥斯特里格的天空

两百米的高空
身体在空中微微颤动
一松手
我在空中俯冲

行走的动物
理解不了的飞的自由
在失控中
迎面扑头

忽然明白了鹰的视角
强劲的风把空气吹成一个透明的球
身体缓缓地迎着气流下降
连绵的绿树海洋在脚下
也在球里缓缓地起伏波动

减去重力
时间变慢
一英里
仿佛一世间

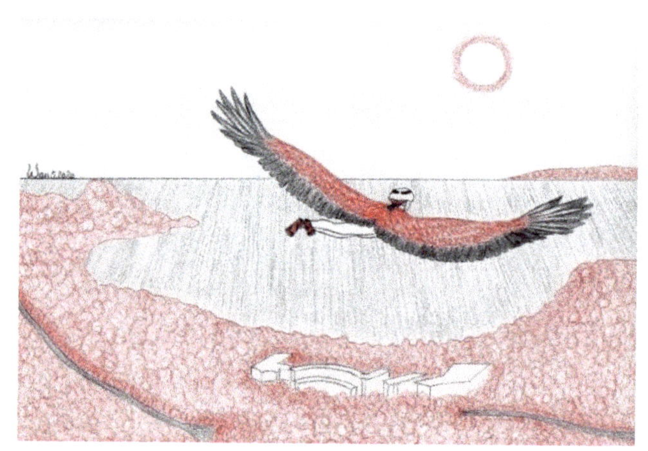

在哥斯特里格像鹰一样飞翔

三　哥斯特里格-不知名的河

船长戴着一顶白色的牛仔帽
黝黑的脸上写满了故事

沿着他的手指往左看
一片泥土的颜色上有些许土包
瞪着眼睛才发现
土包是鳄鱼宝宝
一条两条三条四条
五条六条七条八条
鳄鱼母亲的眼睛浮在河面
默默注视

顺着他的手指往右看
十几个黄色的翅膀在岸上
一群蝴蝶在吮吸泥土里的矿物质

跟着他仰头看树干
那些面具一样的小蘑菇
是躲在树干下面睡觉的蝙蝠

船在河水里静静地漂
只有船长偶尔用他鹰一样的眼睛打破沉默

忽然一阵嘶嘶的吼叫
船长伸长手臂四十五度角
一棵横跨在河面的大树上头
十多个吼猴踩着一个个半圆的弧
从树林的一端荡到另一端
俯瞰威吓着我们这些多余的外来者

在这不知名的河
一位土著船长
一个静静的午后

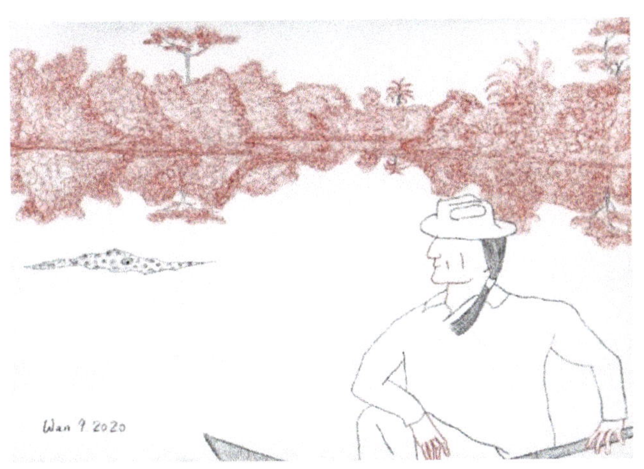

哥斯特里格的船长驾船在一条静静的河上

一　尼加拉瓜这个地方

去过一个地方
于是那个地方不再是一个地名
它有了实实在在的肉身
闻一闻有气味
尝一尝有滋味
形色都会浮现在眼前

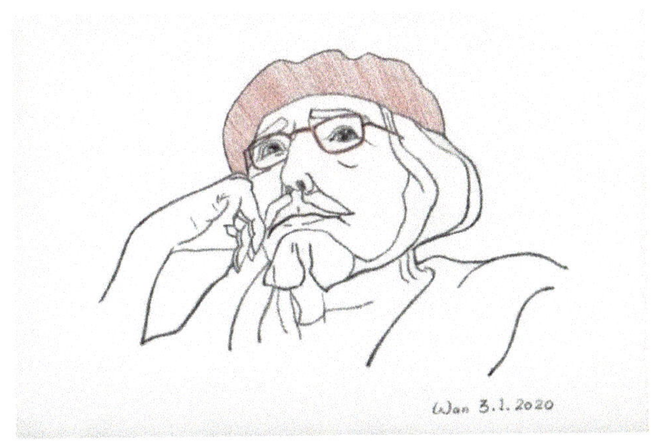

尼加拉瓜诗人 Father Ernesto Cardenal
于二零二零年三月一日去世

二　尼加拉瓜 Apoyo 火山坑湖上的小岛

波澜不惊的湖
光着膀子的渔民回头看看我们
继续撒网

三百六十多个小岛
红瓦白墙木船
年轻人同样摸着电脑上网
只是离开的时候摸的是那橹桨
在咯吱咯吱声中荡到岸边

两万年前的大爆炸
在今天的慢悠悠里找不到踪影
是不是这被水环绕的日子
让那电掣风驰的世界变成了一个游戏
需要的时候拿鱼去换些用品
更多时间活在游戏之外

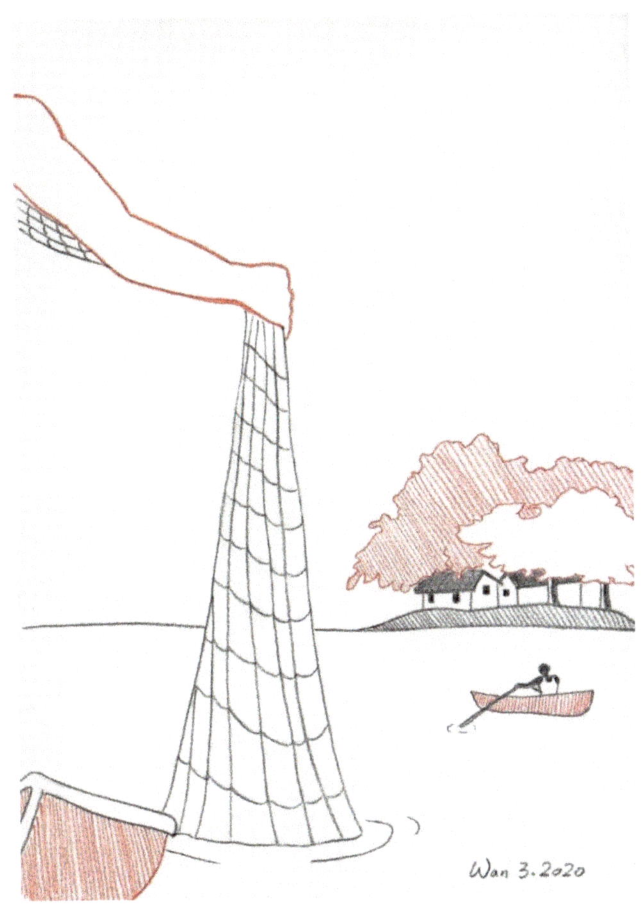

坐船打鱼、购物—生活在尼加拉瓜火山湖的小岛上

第六篇： 上海的月光

故乡的玫瑰色

永远不会褪却

儿时留存的友谊

永远不会忘却

只是大厦越来越高

马路越来越宽

去哪里寻找旧时的记忆

黄浦江的汽笛声

依然引乡愁澎湃

空气中的潮湿

依然勾起故乡的味道

只是高架越来越多

速度越来越快

去哪里回味长大的滋味

在这日新月异的城市

在这不停追逐的城市

是否还有某个放学的午后

两个做完功课的孩子
在弄堂口
等着臭豆腐在小贩的油锅里吱吱地变脆

在这熙熙攘攘的人群里
在这繁花似锦的霓虹间
有什么让你放轻松
知道自己是谁
知道自己在哪里
知道梦是什么
知道热情去追

夸父追不到永恒的太阳
外面的世界永不停下
我的故乡
回头看看傍晚的黄浦江
回头看看夜晚的苏州河
她们静静地流淌了千百年
白色的月光洒落在水面上
宛如一首月光曲
低声唱着心里的伤

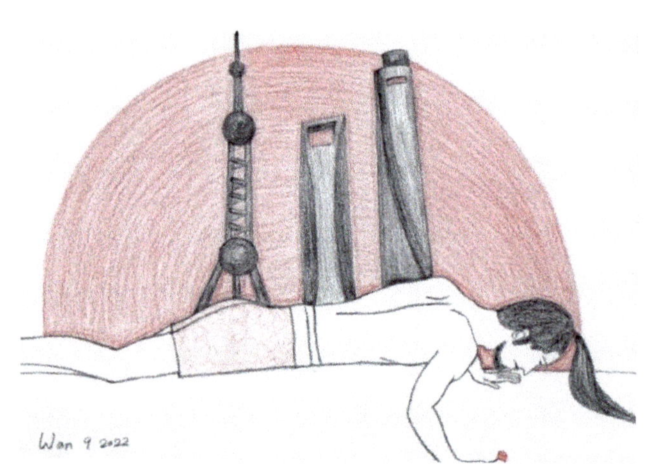

夸父追不到永恒的太阳

一　　寻找玻璃房

济州岛上有一座玻璃房
玻璃房里有一家薄荷餐厅
餐厅里四面是及地的玻璃墙
玻璃墙外是带着朦胧雾气的海
连着海的是传说中的仙山半岛

要寻到这座玻璃房
你得在迷宫般的停车场里找到那个小小的百
货店
百货店里的女孩会带你到店门口
去拍一张手绘的地图
地图的当中写着玻璃房
连蒙带猜找到那扇石头堆成的幸福门
然后就对着地图迷路了
索性放下地图

四处张望
海水润泽的空气中
人的气息在聚集
走着走着
找到了越来越多的同行

走过青草地
走过身上略带土色的白色骏马
走过红心雕像
走过像青蛙的巨大岩石
走过一扇半遮半掩的石墙
玻璃房就矗立在海角上

坐在玻璃房中央
看潮湿的空气遮住了太阳的脸庞
绿色的青草地绕着海边的小道
济州岛露出了北加州的模样
忽然明白了何处是故乡

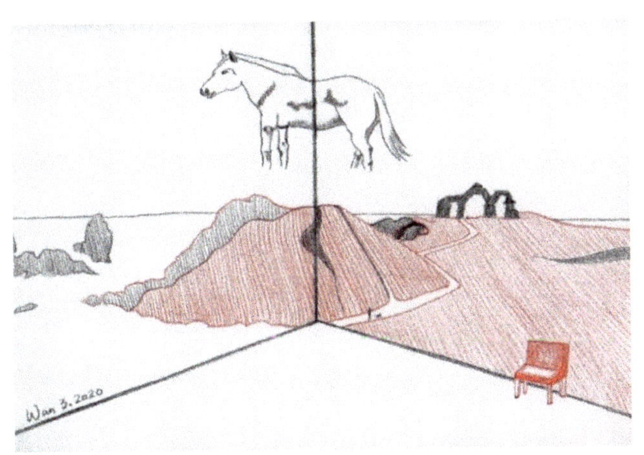

寻找玻璃房—济州岛

二　海边的白色教堂

济州岛的某个海边

站在高高的山崖上

看到人像蚂蚁一般冲浪

沿着草坪的小径漫步

有一个小巧的铜人像

继续走到尽头

一座白色的教堂

花瓣一样的开放

门就这样半开着

轻轻一推

迎面一片白色贝壳叮当作响

白色的落地窗

白色的大钢琴

白色的三层台阶

白色的长条椅

恍惚错入了一场别人的爱情剧场

心，涟漪一样荡漾

笑，花儿一样绽放

站在这白玫瑰的中央

当初那阳光背面的微笑

又揭开白纱

爬上心头

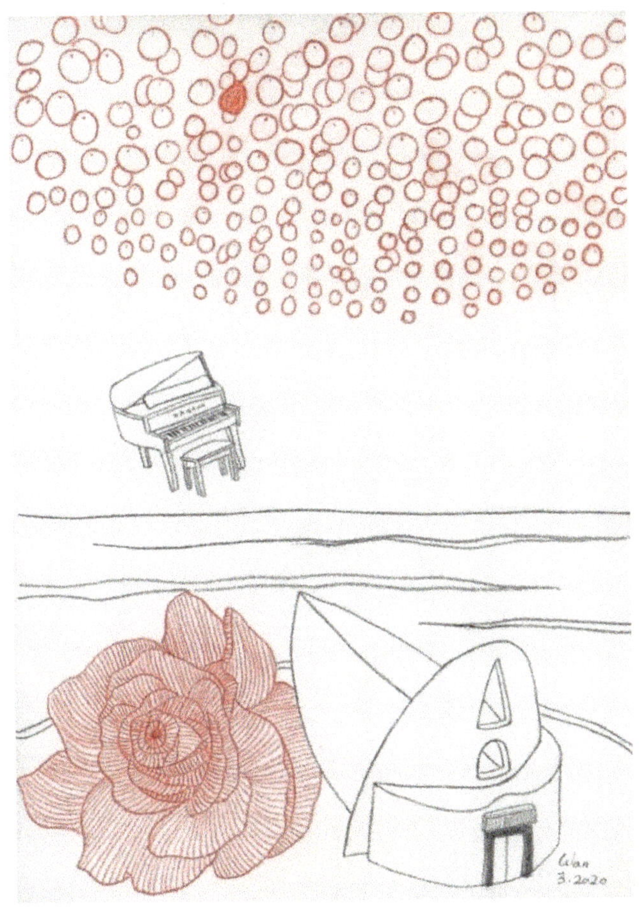

海边的白色教堂

三　导游凯文

黄色马褂
紫色缎裤
导游凯文略微颔首
操一口韩式英文

仁德宫里
他略弓着背
"房子只是一个盒子
珍贵的是里面的文化"

设计中心内
他的眼睛闪亮
"这是梦的组合：
设计和娱乐
城市和自然
现代和未来"

I SEOUL U 的市标前
他忙前忙后地比划指导
"喷泉前面最上照"

Hanok Village 里
旧瓦石墙的弄堂之间
他领我们吃绿筒紫色冰激凌
"许多部爱情电影曾在这里发生"

高高的首尔电塔上
他温柔地坚持
"别错过爱心锁海洋"
果然
一片红色和粉色之间
禁不住买了一把
写上我们的名字
栓在柱子上
然后把钥匙喂给了邮箱

黄色马褂
紫色缎裤
导游凯文
手把手地
传授韩国的浪漫
说好内容重于形式
形式却把心给骗走了

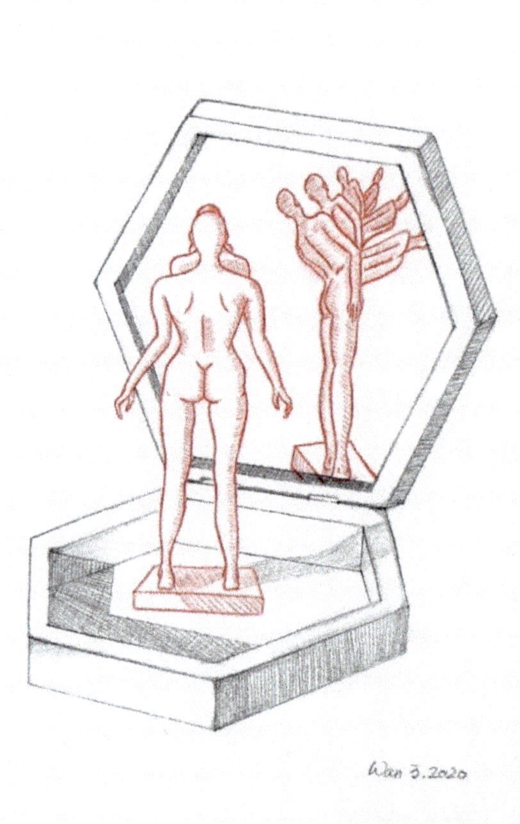

装在盒子里的文化

四　济州岛的海女

在这上海三十八度高温的日子里
济州岛就像一个凉爽的世外桃源
难怪是传说中神仙的所在

济州岛的三宝：风、石头、和海女
风来去于海天之间
石头天长地久地等待
为什么海女
为什么她们依然去海里挖掘
每一天
直到接近生命的终结

因为有一群一起长大的女伴
一起入海一起捕获
一起围着篝火取暖

因为潜入海那静谧的下沉
像是回到了母亲的子宫
一片蓝色
海浪拍打的声音消失了
安静地只有咕噜咕噜

因为一口气撬起鲍鱼
抬头看到的是那个圆圆的竹篮
充满希望

一声尖锐的气鸣之后
终于长嘘一口与空气相连
大口喘气
大口呼吸

来来回回
五个小时的冰冷
换来的是快超过体重的海产品
沉甸甸地载满了全家生活的供给

这样一群不一样的女子
艰辛却异常幸福

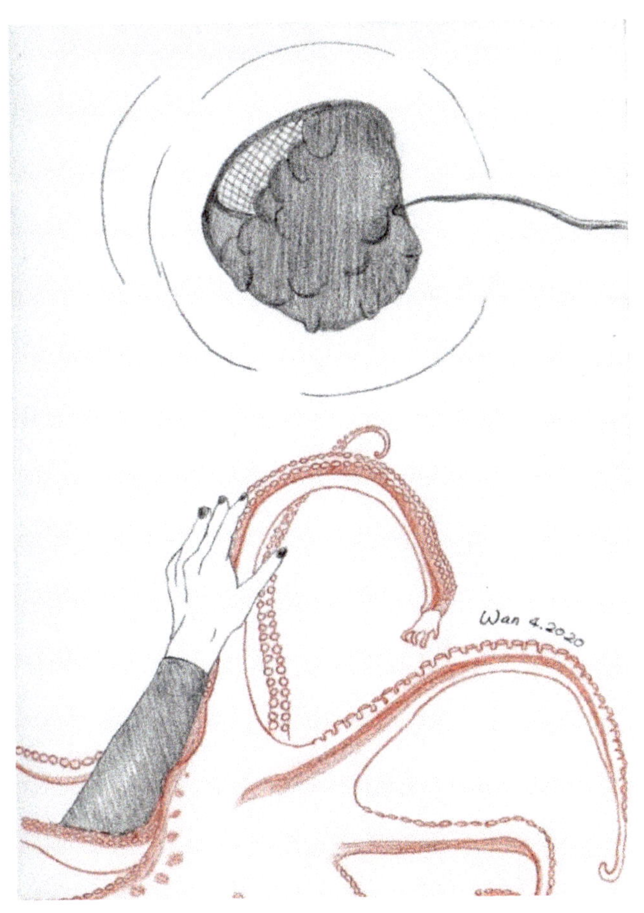

随时生活在未知之中的海女

台湾的故宫

台湾的鼎泰丰

台湾的太鲁阁

台湾的台北 101

台湾的诚品书店

台湾的现代艺术馆

台湾的自由广场

台湾的歌剧院

台湾的士林夜市

台湾的珍珠奶茶

台湾的摩托车

台湾的凤梨酥

台湾的柔软国语

台湾的标准美语

台湾的化缘和尚

台湾的美丽姑娘

台湾的几米漫画

台湾的慢悠悠的蜗蝓文化

台湾的中正堂里写道[4]
生命的意义于生命的延续
生活的目的于生活的提高

千层千面之中
台湾把对人的温情和观世的深邃
不着痕迹地
融在了饮食里
化在了艺术里
像一汪含情脉脉的湖水滋润着人的心脾

就这样被这温存三百六十度地搂抱着
说不出什么特别
却酥了

4　生命的意义在创造宇宙继起之生命；生活的目的在增加人类全体之生活。

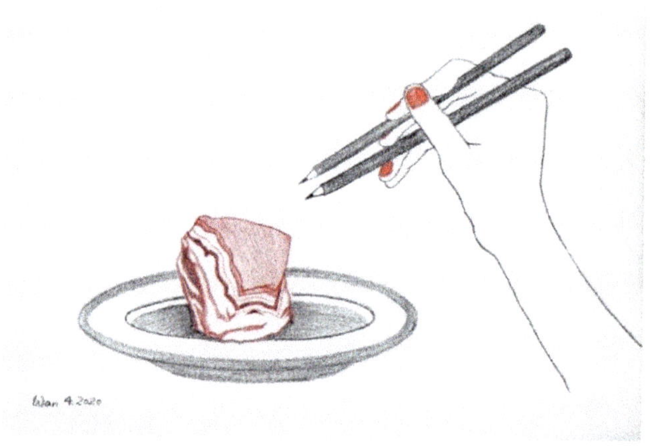

在台湾最好的艺术是食物5，最好的饮食也是艺术

---

5 台湾故宫里的肉形石。

一　　新加坡姐妹一

机场一尘不染地想要把鞋底擦净
海关发的糖果让我们受宠若惊
有条不紊的代价就是明码标价的罚金
这个文明而严厉的国度住着我的亲

一转头彷佛看到七年前
天使一般的她站在栏杆边
我们四眼相锁大声呼喊

七年之后再次相见
时光让我们沉淀
暗流却涌动于大海的平静

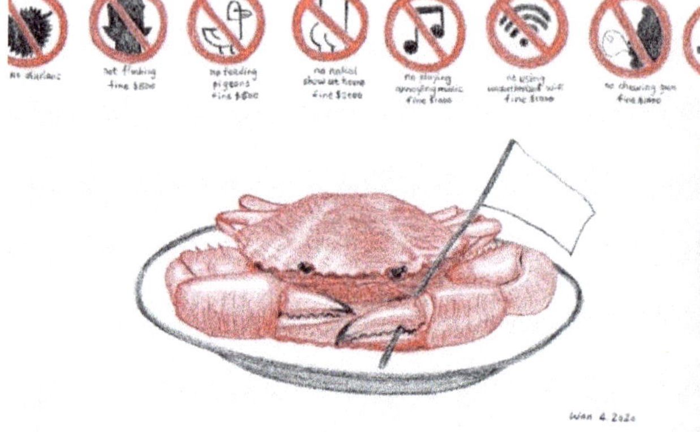

在罚金之城缴械投降的新加坡肉蟹

二　新加坡姐妹二

鸽子一股脑地拔地而起
往回看伊斯兰的宫殿在白光里像神殿一样的
影子
我随影而行的姐妹就在身后
拖着的还有我们爱的小尾巴

我说亲爱的我们一起聊会天吧
她搬来椅子坐下问要说什么

想起 Louis Armstrong 唱着
我看见朋友们一边说你好一边握手
他们其实在说 I love you

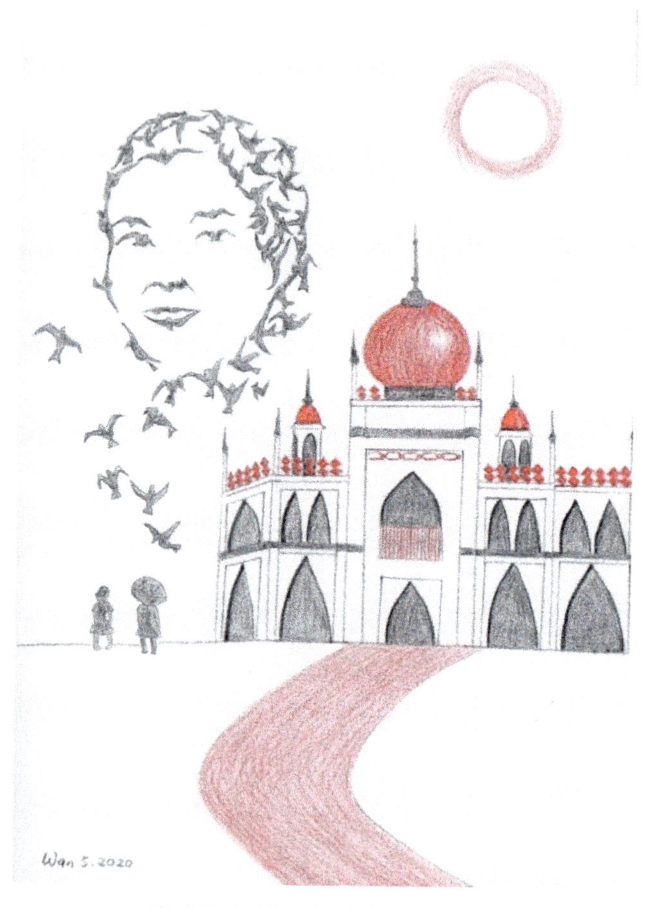

淡淡的问候里藏着友谊的模样

三　新加坡姐妹三

母亲头上的鲜血
写下了世界的敌意
父亲的温文儒雅
吹来不露心绪的春风

孤傲的鱼尾狮
奇异中闪闪发光
喷薄而出的泉水
冷静地拥抱全场
雕像和喷泉之间的对话
回响着狄俄倪索斯的沉醉
和阿波罗的平和

最后说起了故乡
捍卫、忍受、抗议
儿时的路已经写下了今天的争执

是选择爱
还是选择对错
鱼尾狮雕像依然孤傲的站着
喷泉冷静地拥抱全场

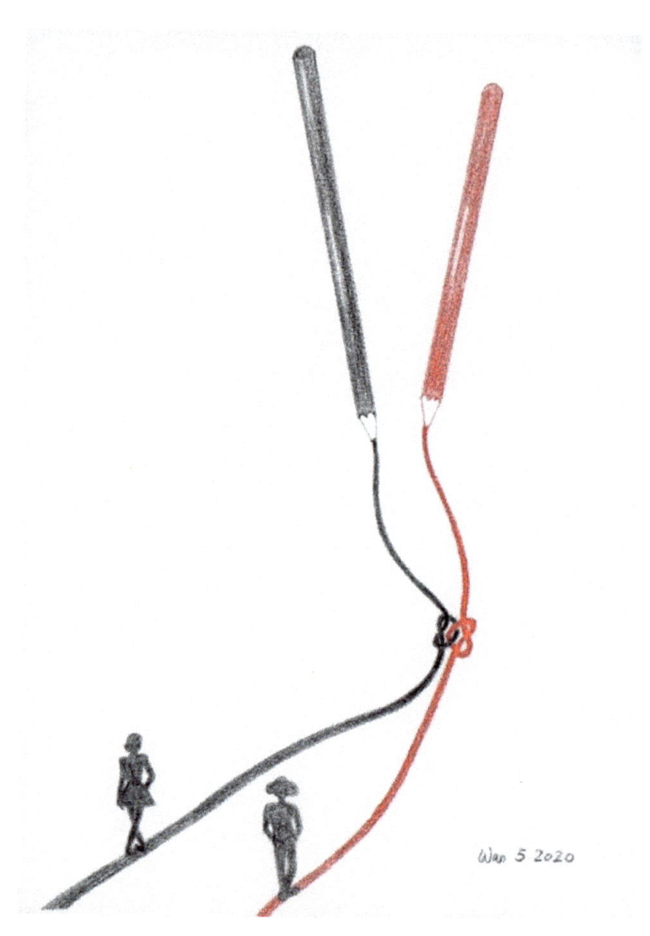

友谊莫不是相似的人天长地久

一　风雨共济后的笑脸

行李在船舱里堆积着
身体在板凳上拥挤着
新加坡的美好就像海市蜃楼一般泯灭
大雨倾泄
我们面无表情地等待着上岸的时刻

板条车把我们拉出了风雨
穿过树林便是我们的住处
海上有宁静的青青石头
屋旁有诱人的蓝色池兜
屋里有日久长情的朋友

鹅黄的灯光
那几张熟悉的脸庞
二十五载的默默流淌
却未改变友谊的模样

安静地听着的
滔滔地述着的
一如既往的安排
毫无倦怠
只让微笑和大笑填满句子间的空白

无论风雨
无论何处
朋友们的笑脸就让生活发了光

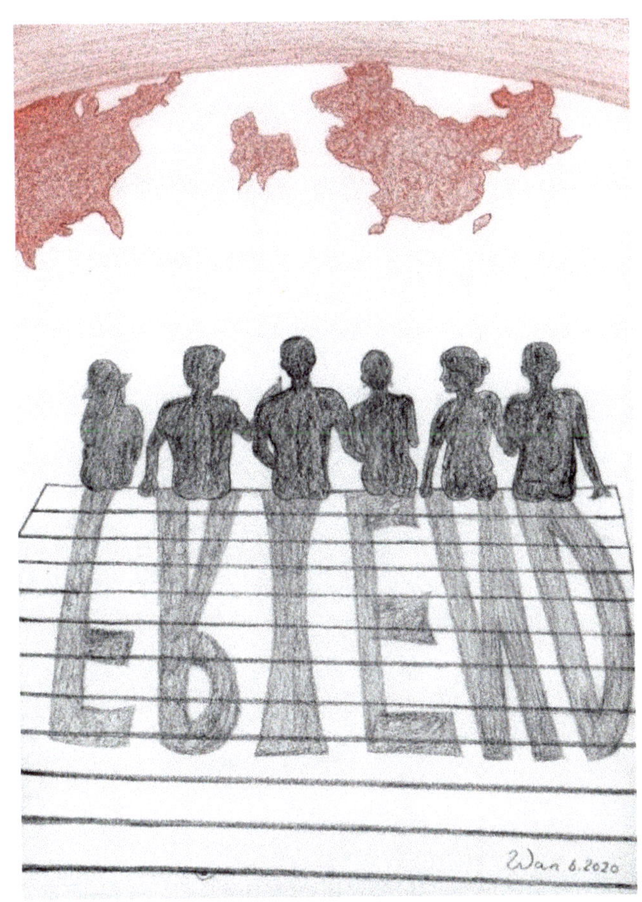

朋 友

二　时光

时光在我们的身体上流过
留下山丘峡谷
时光在我们的面颊上流过
把平湖变成沙漠
时光在我们的心间流过
将爱掩埋于沉默

时光的河流慢慢地流淌
过去从未过去
只是留在了上游
无法追溯遥不可及
却在手指相触瞬间
却在四目相视之间
打开了一扇窗

时光的河流慢慢地流淌
将来已经发生
只是发生在下游
黑暗光明或不可知
却在掌心画上了手纹
却在心间埋下了愿望

像北极星在指引方向

时光的河流慢慢地流淌
现在正骑着白马
深陷河流的当场
无处可躲无处可藏
唯有与它一同呼吸
让感官完全开张
让宇宙扑面而入
让心随波逐浪

一切归于静寂
时光的河流慢慢地流淌

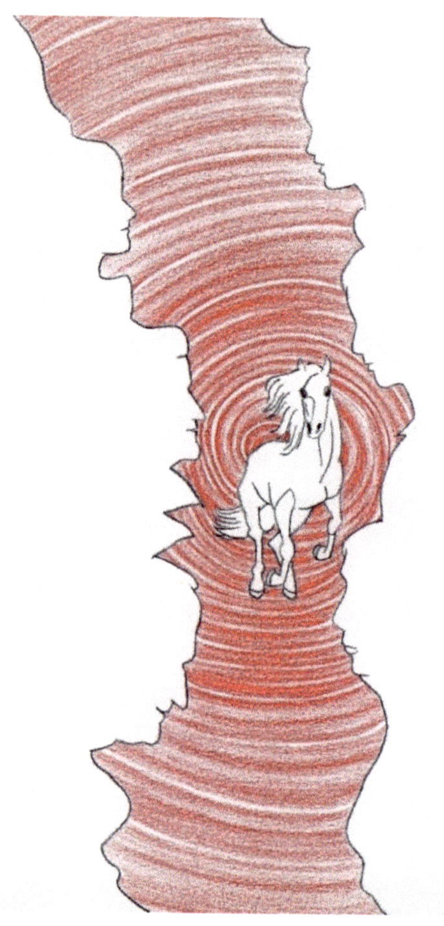

时光的河流

第十一篇： 吉隆坡的红心气球

潮水过后
一片孤寂
唯有贝壳零落在沙滩上

哄哄闹闹
百转千回
才跨入一个全新的国家

窗外双子
杯中黄花
忽闻祈祷的歌悠扬空旷

一日五行
真主在上
虔诚的日子竟让人向往

欲望在下
真理在上
这犹疑人生如何去担当

嬉声笑语
生日快乐
一只红心气球在窗口飘荡
赫然写着
I Love You

心为所动
意志诚服
让爱勾去做优雅的傻瓜

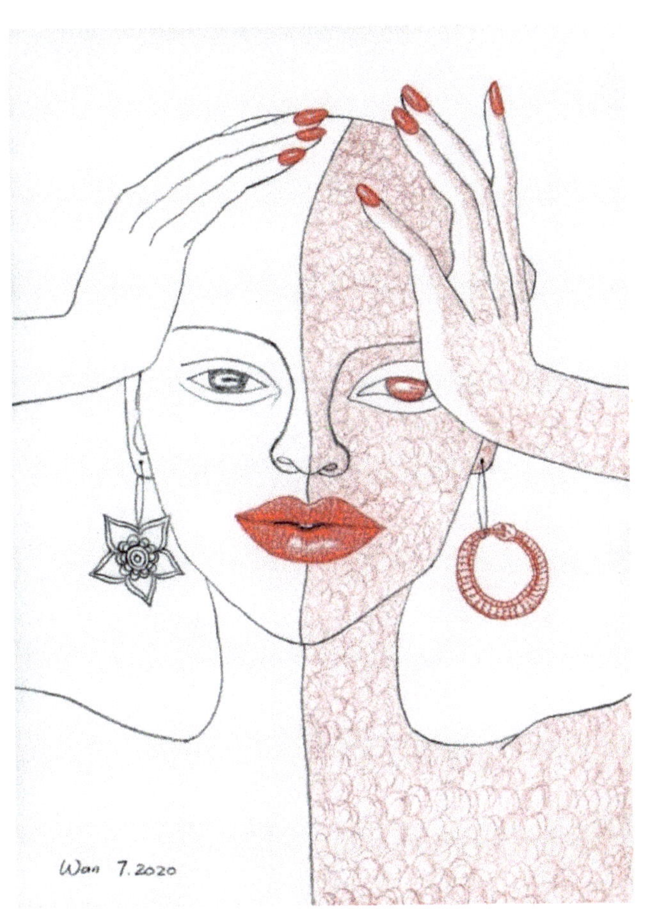

一边是真理一边是欲望

第十二篇： 归程

看不到头的走廊
又闻到了豆浆的香
一碗浓汁绿叶的牛肉面汤
让我们又深陷桃园机场

人不能两次踏入同一条河流
回到同一个地点却能模糊时空

把彼时的我
介绍给此刻的我
忘却的情绪浮上了水面
像失落的花瓣
被一一拾起
遗漏的细节露出了马脚
如出土的文物
被更苍劲的手指轻轻扫开灰尘

现在的我
看着当初的我

你那纤细的触角经历的挫伤
让我用年长的温柔来慢慢疗养
当初的我
看着现在的我
愿我的脆弱真诚和无知
能化解你日益成功的坚强

为什么我们不停地
回到记忆中的地方
因为在那里
两个我的重逢
会发生神奇的变化
又一个我
会被重生

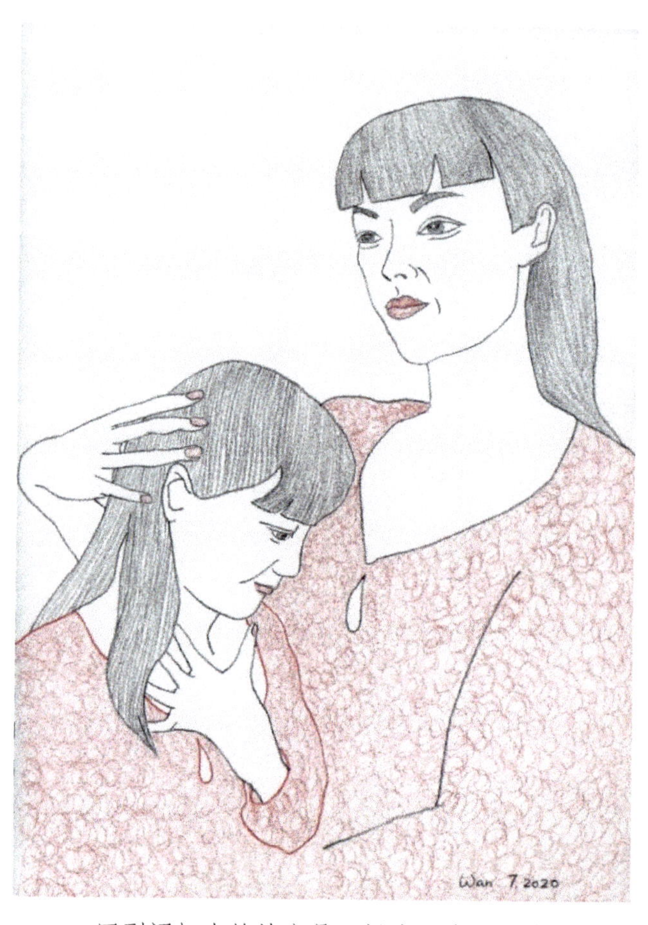

回到记忆中的地方是一场我和我的重逢

第十三篇： 爱德华的双子湖边

一　爱德华的双子湖边

简简单单
干干净净
纯净的蓝天
甜甜的空气
美国就像一个玻璃瓶里的世界

纯粹把嘈杂的感情滤过了
举手投足之间嗅着优良的气息
那些细微的爱意与哀愁
如同消失殆尽

那个让我悲喜的世界
这个让我平和的世界
哪个才真切

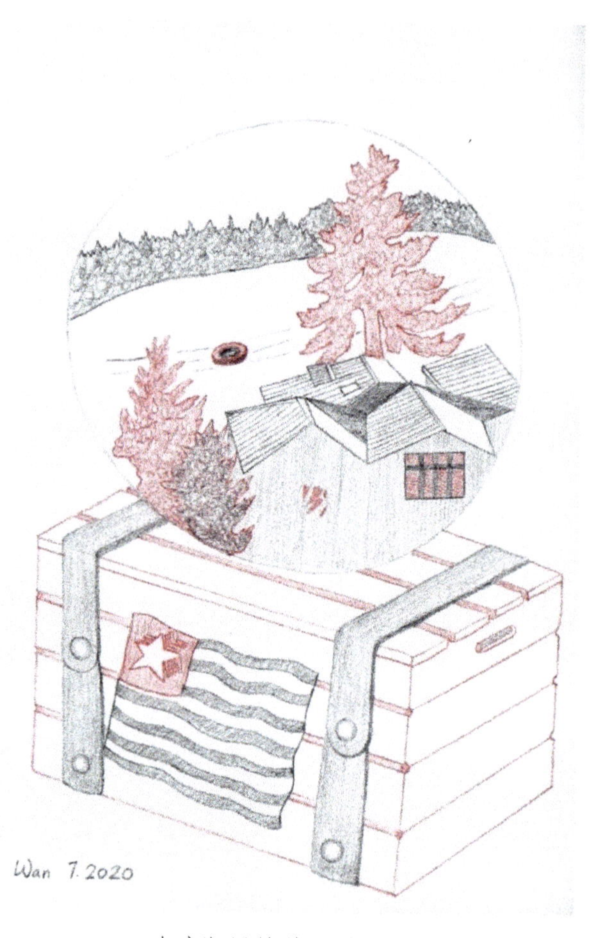

玻璃瓶里的美丽世界

二　远方的朋友

远方的朋友啊
你在那方熙熙攘攘
我在这里朴实无华
我们就这样长啊长
总会长出不一样
这南方的橘
这北方的枳
还牵挂着对方当初的模样

远方的朋友啊
我们像出巢的蜂
去了不同的地方
见了面
可要毫无保留地诉说衷肠
差得越多
耳朵张得越大
我们抑或可想象另一个世界是什么样

远方的朋友啊
虽然我们想
却始终敌不过春去秋来大海茫茫

相思的泪
在心里慢慢流淌
淹没了你的声音
融化了你的笑容
模糊了你的模样

记忆变得更美
却找不到了通往你现在的方向

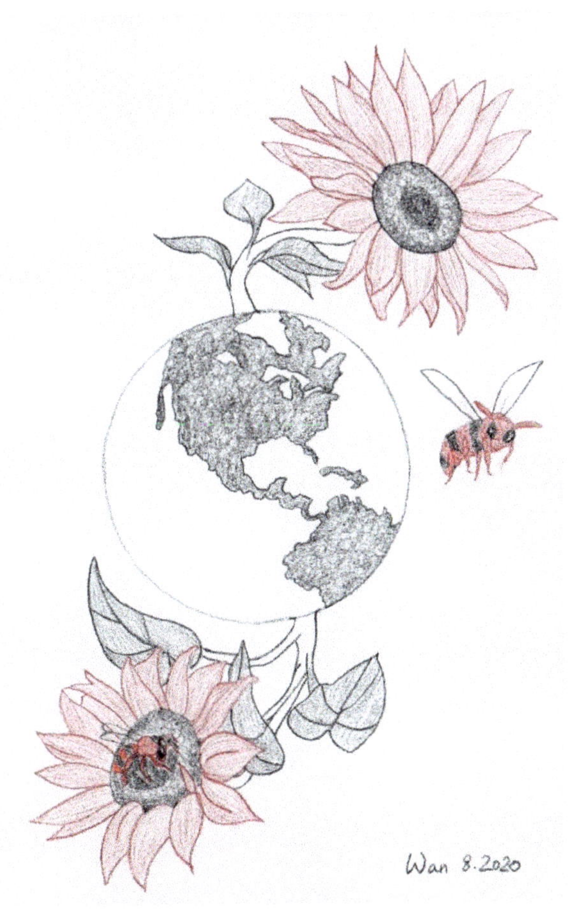

我们像出了巢的蜂去了不同的地方

一　　高速公路边的熊

一觉醒来
猛见高速公路边一只棕熊
神情焦虑
东张西望
我心头一紧
它为什么会出现在这个地方
这么多车来车往

一秒钟后
答案在路上
一头刚被撞死的动物鲜血淋漓
隔着玻璃窗
我可以闻到那新鲜的血肉是一场盛宴
刺激着熊的鼻囊

开着车他问我看到了什么
我说我看到了危险的欲望

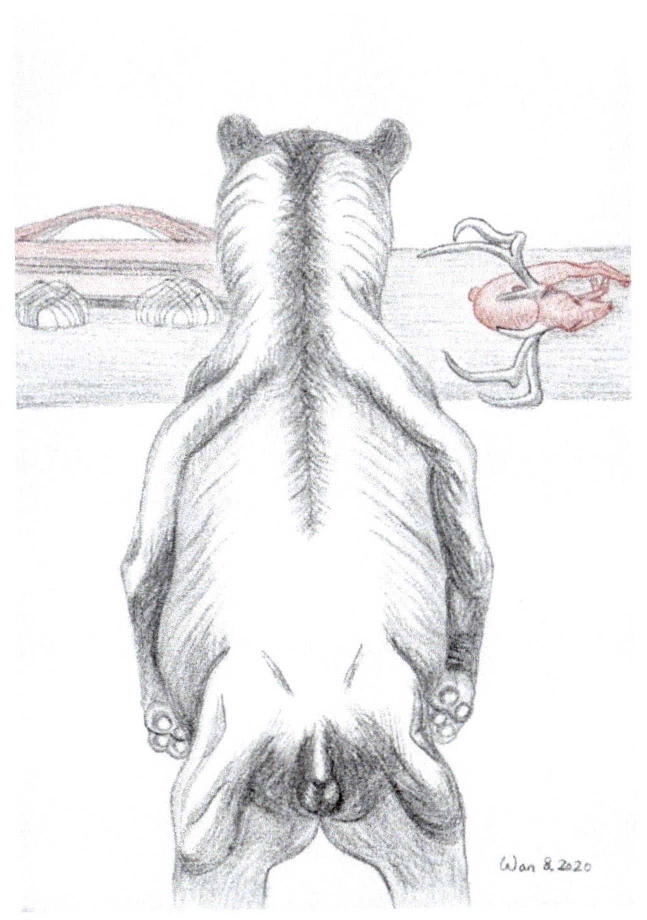

危险的欲望

二 北极星村

泰禾的北极星村满是舒适精美的气味
在这山和树之间像是一个不真实的梦
想起台湾现代艺术馆的时候看到的那个短片
在云南玉田里的废墟里找玉的人在寻找他们
的梦
旁边整齐华丽的别墅区
铃铃作响的吊灯
银色发光的器皿
柔软的席梦思
每天在这里打扫卫生的女人就在这别人的梦
里做一个不相关的人

我们是在找自己的梦
还是在别人的梦里做游人

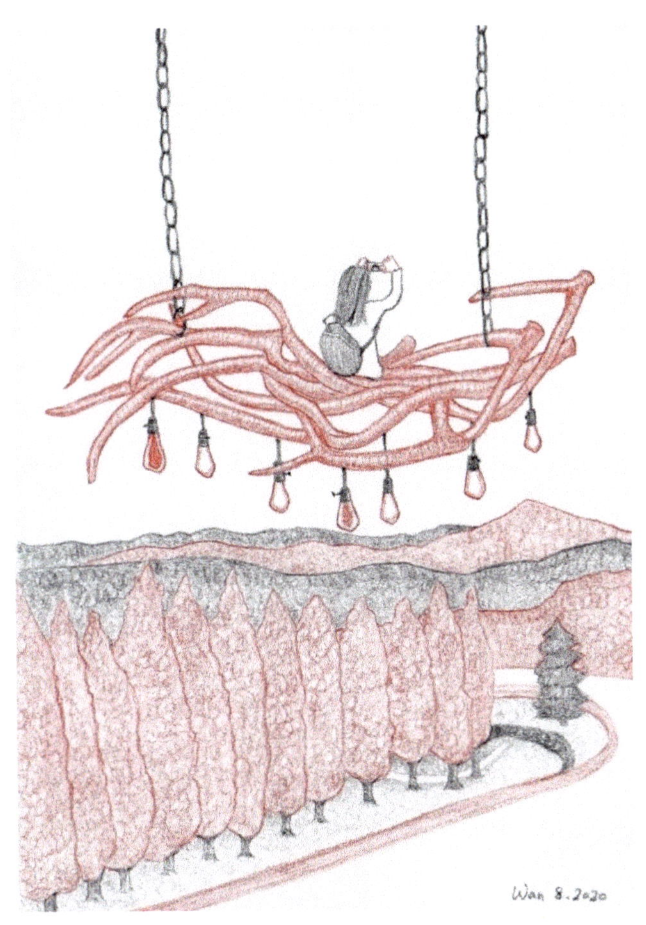

在别人的梦里做游人

第十五篇： 圣地亚哥的奶奶

潮起潮落的失落
在一百岁的奶奶这里抛了锚
挂着一根拐杖
她站在风中优雅如松
光从她雪白的头发透过
照亮我们迷途的眼睛

八十年前
在那个网球属于男人的世界
她用借来的球拍打了个大满贯

七十年前
医生来访
他还有一年的时间
找一份工作吧
带着三个幼小的孩子
年轻的奶奶接下了命运的车轮滚滚

六十年前
系主任的奶奶

批准学生自己搞女性解放活动
却因花花公子杂志送来的三位裸女模特
被传呼到法庭答辩
奶奶不屈不亢实话实说
庭上笑破肚皮
庭下新闻一时

五十年前
前来面试教授的鲍勃
揭开了新的篇章
然而心心相印
改变不了奶奶的意志如钢
每年鲍勃求一次婚
每一次奶奶都说
三个孩子工作太忙
没有时间做新娘
所幸鲍勃同样意志坚强
到了第六年终于鲍勃变成了爷爷
自此开始半个世纪的互诉衷肠

五年前
奶奶和朋友出海翻船
九十多的奶奶和七十多的朋友
一起把船拖回了岸上

三年前
金盆洗手
奶奶终于把网球束高阁之上

一年前
在爱德华的河里玩飞钓
奶奶宣布这是最后一趟

今年
奶奶一如既往
在年度智慧老太6大会上妙语连珠

奶奶是人生剧场上的摇滚明星
台上的她活力四射
台下的我们仰头欣赏

是夜，百岁生日派对落幕
奶奶说
虽然我看不到你们人生的全部
但我知道你们一定会安度

奶奶自然知道
她绽放的人生就是给我们最好的礼物

6　智慧老太（Crones Counsel）：美国一个致力于将年长女性
的价值观介绍给社会的组织。

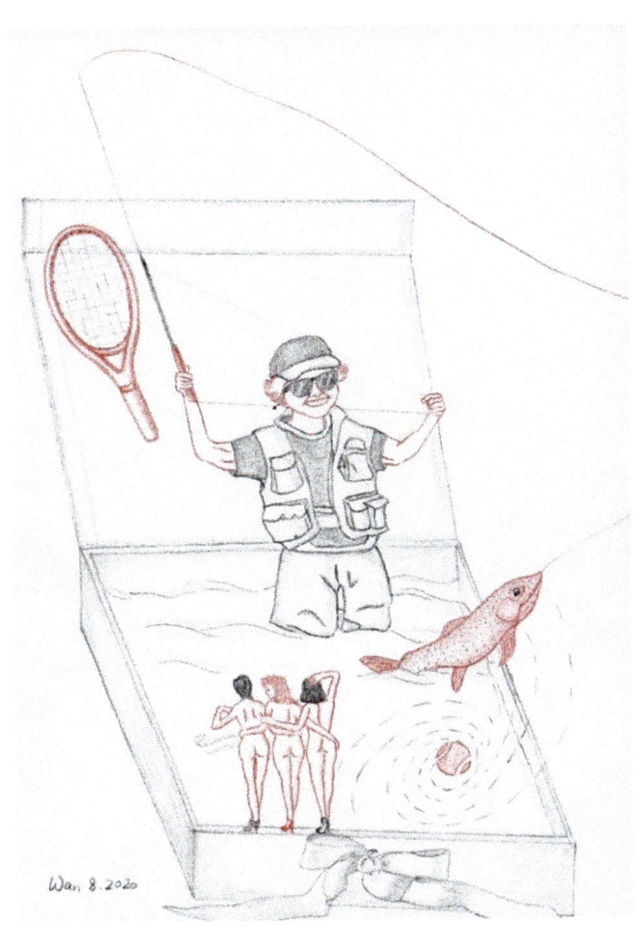

你绽放的人生就是最好的礼物

第十六篇： 回家

加州的空气嗅着富饶
层层叠叠的金色山丘让眼睛写意地笑
路过有老鹰木雕的屋顶和路灯
我疑惑为什么会安在这些地方
直到老鹰呼啦啦张开翅膀飞走了

回到了我思念的地方
毛孔和鼻孔都伸开了懒腰
我像一个每天上紧发条的钟
机械，冷漠，紧张
一个夏天的遗忘
终于卷开了花

用一个夏天去遗忘
日复一日刻下的痕迹统统磨光
露出了我本来的模样
露出了我嘴角边的得意洋洋

用一个夏天去融化
严寒的雪峰

也流出了温柔

用一个夏天回家
那个可以袒胸露腹的地方
枕着草黄的山坡
看着未知的天空
又有了希望

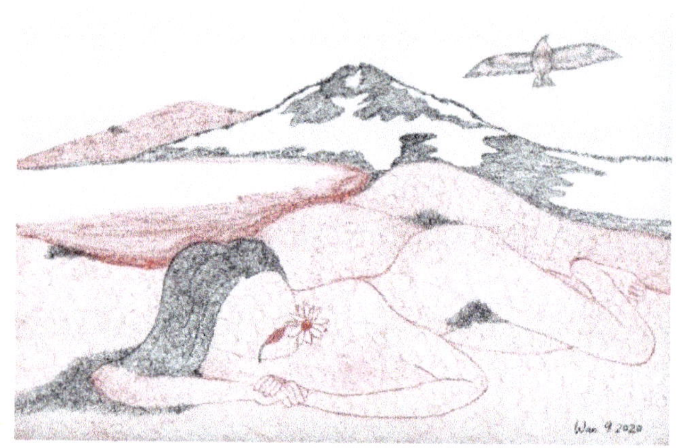

回　家

后　序

　　现在是 2022 年的 10 月，快三年的疫情刚刚开始淡出我们的生活。

　　回过头看，非常庆幸我们遵守了自己的诺言，没有因为先生未能按计划入学麻醉师硕士学位而推迟这次旅行——八个月后这场影响全球的疫情将把我们牢牢地锁在家中。生活大师托尼·罗宾斯曾说过："完美是最低的标准。"没有完美的情况。只有在大致平衡的状态下行动并接受可能的风险，才能继续生长。回到湾区后，先生在度假房产业开启了他真正热爱的、属于他自己的事业。在离开了亚特兰的金融科技上市公司后，我选择了一家位于湾区，为自闭症儿童提供医疗服务的机构，做管理工作。同时我继续夜间的创作，完成了两本儿童插画，并在诗歌的领域里继续探索，构建自己的文字。

　　回顾而言，这次旅行是我人生路上从生理到心灵的一次重启。在这个过程中，我记忆最深刻的竟是出发前三星期，向上司辞行那一刻的忐忑。那是一个为了自己的需要而发声的瞬间，一个脆弱而需要勇气的时刻，也恰好是某种固化的自我开始坍塌的开始。人从生来的柔软到离开世界时的僵硬，是一个生理和精神的固化过程。在追求物质和生活富足和稳定的时候，那些成就我们的也是固化我们的。离开那个熟悉的环境，让自己从肌肉到思维完全脱离了惯性的压力，让它们恢复本来的形状，是一个需要时间的过程。

这次旅行是一项长期计划的结果。我们提前一年就安排了整个旅行的所有行程。利用搬回湾区的机会旅行的想法，在搬去东部前就萌了芽。由于先生精心计算，旅行支出也与平时预算相当。记得刚搬去亚特兰大时，家具晚到了一个多星期。我们坐在地板上，仅有的家当是一张床垫、一个落地灯、两把宜家的红色塑料转椅，几个碗和一把铁锅，却发现生活可以照样继续而并未有大不同。旅行的三个月，所有的家当是两个 40 寸的旅行箱和一把简易的儿童车，我们却度过了最愉快的时光。物质需求是牵绊旅行决定的原因，却往往不是真正的原因；而一旦跨出了这一步，所收获的体验如换羽重生。

尼采说过："生命中最难的阶段，不是没有人懂你，而是你不懂你自己。"愿你我都在寻找自己的路程上，走得踏实、放松与平和。

European customer data cannot be transferred to regions that lack equivalent data protection laws, while China's Cybersecurity Law imposes strict data localization requirements. To navigate these complexities, organizations must work closely with cloud providers to define geographic data boundaries, apply geofencing controls, and ensure that cloud workloads comply with regional data protection laws.

The role of cloud service providers in compliance management is another critical consideration. While major cloud providers such as AWS, Microsoft Azure, and Google Cloud offer built-in security and compliance tools, businesses cannot rely solely on cloud vendors to ensure full compliance. Cloud providers offer security certifications (ISO 27001, SOC 2, FedRAMP, PCI DSS, etc.), automated compliance frameworks, and data protection services, but customers are ultimately responsible for configuring their cloud environments correctly. Misconfigured cloud resources, unrestricted storage buckets, and weak identity access policies remain some of the most common compliance violations, even when using a compliant cloud provider. Organizations must take an active role in security governance, regularly assess their cloud configurations, and enforce security best practices to prevent compliance failures.

Another rising concern in cloud compliance is AI governance and ethical data use. As businesses increasingly integrate artificial intelligence and machine learning into their cloud environments, new compliance challenges arise regarding algorithmic fairness, data privacy, and AI security. Many governments are introducing AI regulatory frameworks to ensure that automated decision-making processes remain transparent, unbiased, and secure. Organizations leveraging AI in the cloud must implement ethical AI practices, conduct algorithm audits, and ensure compliance with emerging AI governance laws to mitigate legal and reputational risks.

Human error remains one of the most significant compliance risks in cloud security. Despite implementing advanced security tools, many compliance violations occur due to employee mistakes, misconfigurations, and poor security awareness. Businesses must prioritize security awareness training, phishing simulations, and cloud compliance workshops to educate employees, IT teams, and developers on data protection policies, cloud security best practices, and regulatory requirements. Compliance should be a shared responsibility across all departments, ensuring that security-conscious behavior becomes an integral part of daily cloud operations.

9.1 The Role of Compliance as a Business Differentiator in Cloud Security

While regulatory compliance is often viewed as a legal obligation, it is increasingly becoming a competitive advantage for businesses operating in cloud environments. Customers, investors, and business partners are prioritizing security and data protection when selecting cloud service providers, and organizations that demonstrate strong compliance practices gain trust, enhance brand reputation, and differentiate themselves in the market. Compliance certifications such as ISO 27001, SOC 2, GDPR compliance, and PCI DSS serve as validation that a company is committed to protecting sensitive information and maintaining high-security standards.

Many businesses that operate in highly regulated industries such as finance, healthcare, and e-commerce must meet stringent security and privacy requirements. Achieving compliance with industry-specific standards such as HIPAA for healthcare, FINRA for financial services, and FedRAMP for government cloud services enables businesses to expand into new markets, secure enterprise partnerships, and unlock growth opportunities. Cloud security compliance is no longer just a requirement for avoiding penalties, it is a strategic business enabler that helps organizations establish credibility and gain a competitive edge over less secure competitor.

Moreover, as consumers become more conscious of data privacy rights, businesses that proactively communicate their commitment to compliance and ethical data handling are more likely to attract and retain customers. Transparency in security policies, clear privacy statements, and regular third-party security audits build customer confidence and reinforce trust. Companies that implement privacy-by-design principles ensuring that security and compliance are integrated into every stage of cloud deployment are better positioned to navigate regulatory changes and maintain long-term customer loyalty.

9.2 Overcoming the Compliance Challenges of Emerging Cloud Technologies

As cloud computing evolves, new technologies such as edge computing, serverless architectures, and blockchain solutions introduce fresh compliance challenges. Organizations must stay ahead of changing regulatory landscapes, adapt their compliance frameworks, and ensure that innovative cloud solutions meet security requirements without compromising operational efficiency.

Edge computing, which distributes data processing across multiple locations closer to the end user, raises concerns about data sovereignty and regulatory compliance. Since edge devices and computing nodes may be deployed across different jurisdictions, businesses must ensure that data residency requirements are met while maintaining strong security controls across decentralized cloud environments. Unlike traditional cloud models where data storage and processing occur in centralized data centers, edge computing requires adaptive security policies that account for geographically dispersed workloads, local data encryption, and secure data transmission protocols.

Serverless computing, which allows businesses to deploy applications without managing underlying infrastructure, presents another compliance challenge. While serverless platforms offer agility and cost efficiency, they often abstract security controls from the customer, increasing reliance on cloud providers for security enforcement. Organizations must ensure that serverless applications comply with regulatory requirements, particularly when handling customer data, financial transactions, or healthcare records. Implementing cloud-native security controls, API security monitoring, and automated compliance testing is essential to maintaining visibility and control over serverless cloud deployments.

Additionally, blockchain technology is emerging as a potential compliance solution by providing immutable, tamper-proof audit logs for cloud environments. Blockchain-based compliance solutions enable businesses to prove data integrity, verify security events, and demonstrate regulatory adherence in a transparent and cryptographically secure manner. However, businesses must also consider legal and ethical implications, such as the challenges of GDPR's right to be forgotten conflicting with blockchain's immutable nature. Organizations leveraging blockchain for compliance purposes must explore privacy-enhancing technologies, such as zero-knowledge proofs and confidential computing, to strike a balance between security, transparency, and regulatory obligations.

Cloud compliance is no longer just about meeting minimum security standards, it is an essential component of business resilience, market differentiation, and long-term success in a cloud-driven economy. Organizations that integrate compliance into their overall cloud security strategy will not only avoid legal and financial risks but also gain customer trust, improve operational security, and drive business growth. As cloud technology continues to evolve, businesses must adopt adaptive compliance frameworks, leverage AI-driven compliance automation, and stay informed about emerging regulatory changes to ensure continuous adherence to industry standards.

Compliance is an ongoing journey, not a one-time achievement. Organizations must continuously assess their security posture, enhance governance frameworks, and invest in security awareness training to foster a culture of compliance and security-first thinking. By embracing privacy-by-design, ethical AI practices, and transparent security policies, businesses can future-proof their cloud environments, maintain regulatory integrity, and position themselves as trusted leaders in cloud security.

Chapter 10
The Future of Cloud Security

As cloud computing continues to evolve, the future of cloud security will be shaped by emerging technologies, evolving cyber threats, regulatory advancements, and the increasing reliance on automation and artificial intelligence. Organizations must prepare for a rapidly changing security landscape, where traditional security models will no longer be sufficient to protect dynamic, distributed, and highly interconnected cloud environments. The need for proactive threat intelligence, AI-driven security automation, and decentralized security architectures will define the next generation of cloud security strategies. Businesses that embrace innovation, adopt a forward-thinking approach, and continuously refine their security frameworks will be better positioned to mitigate cyber risks, maintain regulatory compliance, and ensure resilience against future threats.

One of the most significant transformations in cloud security will be the expansion of Zero Trust Architecture (ZTA) as the default security model. With the disappearance of traditional network perimeters, organizations must move beyond implicit trust and enforce continuous verification, strict access controls, and identity-based authentication mechanisms for every user, device, and workload accessing cloud resources. Zero Trust will become more granular and adaptive, leveraging AI-driven risk assessments and real-time behavioral analytics to dynamically adjust security policies based on contextual factors such as user behavior, device security posture, and geographic location. Businesses will increasingly adopt Zero Trust Network Access (ZTNA) solutions, replacing traditional VPNs with more secure, identity-aware access mechanisms that minimize attack surfaces and prevent lateral movement in cloud environments.

Another critical development in cloud security is the integration of AI and machine learning to enhance threat detection, automate incident response, and predict emerging attack patterns. AI-driven security solutions will play a pivotal role in identifying sophisticated cyber threats, analyzing massive datasets in real-time, and autonomously responding to security incidents with minimal human intervention. Machine learning algorithms will enable security platforms to detect anomalies, distinguish between normal and suspicious activity, and predict potential security vulnerabilities before they are exploited. AI-powered security automation will also accelerate forensic investigations, optimize security operations, and reduce response times to cyber incidents, making cloud security more efficient and adaptive.

As organizations continue to move toward decentralized and multi-cloud environments, security models must evolve to protect workloads across diverse cloud platforms, edge computing environments, and hybrid infrastructures. Decentralized cloud security architectures will emerge, leveraging technologies such as blockchain, confidential computing, and secure multi-party computation (SMPC) to ensure data integrity, enhance privacy, and prevent unauthorized tampering. Blockchain-based security solutions will provide transparent, immutable audit logs, allowing organizations to track security events and ensure compliance with regulatory requirements in a verifiable and tamper-proof manner. Confidential computing, which enables data encryption even during processing, will become a foundational technology for securing sensitive workloads in the cloud.

The rise of quantum computing presents both opportunities and challenges for cloud security. While quantum computing has the potential to revolutionize data processing and cryptographic computations, it also poses a significant threat to traditional encryption algorithms. Many of today's widely used cryptographic methods, such as RSA and ECC encryption, could become obsolete in the face of quantum-powered attacks. Organizations must begin preparing for the post-quantum security era, adopting quantum-resistant encryption algorithms to safeguard cloud-stored data from future threats. Governments, security researchers, and technology companies are already working on post-quantum cryptographic standards, and businesses must stay ahead of these developments to future-proof their cloud security infrastructure.

Another emerging challenge in cloud security is the increased risk of supply chain attacks targeting cloud service providers, third-party vendors, and software dependencies. Attackers are shifting their focus to compromising cloud-based software supply chains, injecting malicious code into widely used cloud applications, APIs, and infrastructure components. Security by Design and Secure Software Development Lifecycle (SDLC) practices will become essential in mitigating supply chain risks, ensuring that every stage of cloud application development and deployment is protected from malicious exploitation. Organizations must implement continuous security testing, code signing, and third-party risk assessments to prevent supply chain compromises and ensure the integrity of cloud services.

The future of cloud security will also be influenced by the growing adoption of privacy-enhancing technologies (PETs), such as homomorphic encryption, differential privacy, and federated learning. These technologies will enable businesses to process and analyze data while preserving user privacy, reducing regulatory risks, and ensuring compliance with stringent data protection laws. Homomorphic encryption allows computations to be performed on encrypted data without decryption, enabling secure data analytics and AI model training without exposing sensitive information. Federated learning enables machine learning models to be trained across multiple decentralized datasets while keeping raw data private, reducing security and privacy risks in cloud-based AI applications.

Regulatory compliance will continue to shape the future of cloud security, with governments enforcing stricter data protection laws, cybersecurity mandates, and industry-specific security frameworks. Businesses must stay ahead of evolving regulatory requirements, adopting automated compliance management solutions that continuously monitor security policies, enforce access controls, and generate real-time compliance reports. The convergence of AI-driven compliance automation and cloud-native security governance frameworks will help organizations maintain regulatory alignment, reduce compliance burdens, and avoid costly penalties for non-compliance with global data privacy laws.

The human factor in cloud security will remain a crucial element, as cybersecurity awareness, employee training, and security culture continue to be key drivers of cloud resilience. While automation and AI-powered security solutions will reduce manual security tasks, human oversight, strategic decision-making, and security leadership will always be essential. Organizations must invest in security awareness programs, ethical AI training, and continuous skills development for cybersecurity professionals to stay ahead of emerging threats and build a security-first mindset across all levels of the business.

As cloud security enters a new era of AI-powered automation, quantum-resistant cryptography, and decentralized security architectures, businesses must adopt a forward-looking approach to cybersecurity. The organizations that embrace innovation, proactively adapt to new security challenges, and integrate advanced security frameworks into their cloud strategy will be best positioned to protect digital assets, secure cloud environments, and maintain trust in an increasingly interconnected and data-driven world.

Cloud security is no longer an option; it is a necessity for businesses navigating the complexities of a digital-first world. The future of cloud security will be shaped by continuous technological advancements, evolving regulatory landscapes, and an ever-expanding threat landscape. Businesses that invest in cutting-edge security solutions, integrate AI-driven threat detection, and embrace Zero Trust security models will be better equipped to detect, prevent, and respond to cyber threats in real time.

The key to long-term cloud security resilience lies in continuous adaptation, proactive risk management, and a strong cybersecurity culture. Organizations must stay informed, agile, and committed to evolving their security strategies to keep pace with the rapidly changing cybersecurity landscape. By embracing next-generation security technologies, regulatory compliance best practices, and AI-powered automation, businesses can secure their cloud environments, protect sensitive data, and build a trusted foundation for the digital future.

The evolution of cloud security is not just about responding to threats but about anticipating and preventing them before they materialize. Businesses must move beyond reactive security models and embrace predictive security analytics, where AI-driven systems continuously analyze security logs, user behavior, and global threat intelligence to forecast potential attack scenarios. This shift from detection to prevention will enable organizations to stay ahead of attackers rather than simply responding to breaches after they occur. The integration of self-learning security models will allow cloud security platforms to evolve in real-time, adapting to new vulnerabilities, attack techniques, and emerging compliance requirements without manual intervention.

As cloud environments become more distributed and complex, security operations will need to function at scale, requiring the orchestration of multiple security technologies across hybrid, multi-cloud, and edge computing infrastructures. Cloud security strategies must extend beyond traditional data centers and centralized cloud providers, incorporating security controls for IoT devices, 5G networks, and decentralized cloud services. Organizations must prepare for a future where security perimeters no longer exist, and data protection must be enforced at every access point, no matter where the data resides.

One of the most critical aspects of future cloud security will be trust management in autonomous systems and AI-driven decision-making. As AI takes on a larger role in automated threat detection, policy enforcement, and security governance, businesses must ensure that AI-powered security solutions remain transparent, ethical, and unbiased. Organizations will need to develop explainable AI (XAI) security frameworks, allowing security teams to understand, interpret, and verify AI-driven security decisions. The rise of autonomous security agents—AI-powered security tools that can detect and neutralize cyber threats without human intervention—will require new levels of accountability, governance, and oversight to prevent unintended security actions and biases.

Another transformative trend in cloud security is the convergence of cybersecurity and cloud-native DevSecOps. Security will no longer be a separate layer applied after development, but instead, it will be embedded into every stage of the software development lifecycle (SDLC). DevSecOps will enable businesses to integrate security best practices directly into cloud application development, automating security testing, vulnerability scanning, and compliance validation before applications are deployed. This shift towards proactive security engineering will ensure that cloud applications are secure by design, reducing the risk of misconfigurations, exploitable vulnerabilities, and unauthorized access in production environments.

As quantum computing progresses, the cloud security industry must also prepare for the quantum threat era, where advanced quantum algorithms could break current cryptographic standards, rendering traditional encryption useless. Organizations must begin transitioning to quantum-resistant cryptographic algorithms and exploring post-quantum security frameworks to safeguard sensitive cloud data from future quantum attacks. Security researchers and cloud providers are already working on post-quantum encryption standards, and businesses that start implementing quantum-safe security protocols now will have a significant advantage in future-proofing their cloud environments.

The role of collaborative threat intelligence in cloud security will also expand, with organizations, governments, and cloud providers sharing security insights, attack data, and vulnerability reports to create a unified defense against cybercriminals. As cyber threats grow more sophisticated, businesses will need to leverage collective intelligence, AI-driven threat hunting, and global security alliances to stay ahead of nation-state actors, ransomware groups, and cloud-based malware threats. Organizations that participate in threat-sharing networks, security consortiums, and real-time cyber intelligence exchanges will be better equipped to detect, respond to, and neutralize security threats at scale.

Another significant aspect of the future of cloud security is the rise of self-healing cloud security architectures, where cloud systems are designed to automatically detect security risks, reconfigure defenses, and recover from cyber incidents without human intervention. Self-healing security frameworks will use AI-driven anomaly detection, real-time risk assessment, and automated remediation workflows to strengthen cloud resilience. These intelligent security systems will identify weak points, deploy security patches, and restore cloud workloads autonomously, minimizing the risk of data breaches, system failures, and cyberattacks.

Businesses must not only invest in cutting-edge security tools but also cultivate a cybersecurity culture that promotes continuous learning, awareness, and collaboration. Human expertise will remain a critical component of cloud security, as security professionals must work alongside AI-driven security tools to make informed decisions, oversee automated security operations, and ensure ethical implementation of cybersecurity technologies. Organizations that foster a strong security-first mindset, invest in workforce training, and prioritize security governance will be in the best position to navigate the future of cloud security with confidence and agility.

The next decade of cloud security will be defined by automation, intelligence, and resilience. Businesses that embrace Zero Trust principles, adopt AI-driven security automation, and prepare for the quantum computing era will be well-positioned to defend against evolving cyber threats, secure their digital assets, and maintain trust in an increasingly interconnected world. Cloud security is no longer just about protecting data, it is about enabling innovation, ensuring business continuity, and building a secure foundation for the digital economy of the future.

10.1 The Convergence of AI and Human-Led Security in Cloud Protection

While AI and automation are set to dominate the future of cloud security, human expertise remains irreplaceable. The most effective security strategies will not be based solely on machine-driven automation, but on a harmonious blend of AI-driven analytics and human oversight. AI can process vast amounts of security data, detect patterns, and respond to threats at machine speed, but security professionals provide critical thinking, contextual decision-making, and ethical judgment, qualities that AI lacks.

In the evolving cybersecurity landscape, AI will serve as an assistant, not a replacement, for human security analysts. Security teams will rely on AI-driven Security Information and Event Management (SIEM) platforms, predictive threat intelligence, and automated response mechanisms to handle routine security tasks, while reserving high-risk, complex, and strategic security decisions for human intervention. The role of cybersecurity professionals will shift from manual threat detection and response to AI oversight, strategic risk assessment, and security architecture design.

Moreover, ethical considerations in AI-driven security will require human judgment. AI-driven security models, while powerful, can introduce biases, misclassify threats, or generate false positives, leading to over-restrictive security controls that disrupt legitimate business operations. Human oversight ensures that security decisions align with ethical guidelines, business priorities, and regulatory requirements. Organizations will need to invest in AI governance frameworks, security ethics training, and explainable AI (XAI) models to maintain transparency, fairness, and accountability in AI-powered cloud security.

10.2 Decentralized Security and the Role of Blockchain in Cloud Protection

As cyber threats become more sophisticated, organizations are exploring decentralized security architectures that remove single points of failure from cloud environments. One of the most promising developments in this area is blockchain-based security solutions, which leverage distributed ledgers, cryptographic integrity, and tamper-proof audit trails to enhance cloud protection.

Blockchain technology is particularly valuable in ensuring data integrity and preventing unauthorized modifications. In traditional cloud security models, logs, configurations, and access control records are stored in centralized databases, which can be altered, deleted, or manipulated by malicious insiders or attackers. By recording security logs and access events on an immutable blockchain ledger, businesses can guarantee the authenticity and verifiability of security data, reducing the risk of insider attacks and unauthorized tampering.

Additionally, blockchain-powered identity management systems are emerging as a decentralized alternative to traditional IAM (Identity and Access Management) solutions. In these systems, users maintain control over their digital identities using self-sovereign identity (SSI) frameworks, where authentication credentials are stored securely on a blockchain and verified without relying on a central identity provider. This eliminates the risks associated with credential theft, password reuse, and centralized identity breaches, making cloud authentication more secure and privacy centric.

Smart contracts, self-executing agreements stored on a blockchain can also automate security enforcement in cloud environments. Businesses can program security policies, compliance rules, and access controls into smart contracts, ensuring that only authorized actions are executed based on predefined security parameters. If a security violation occurs, smart contracts can trigger automated incident response mechanisms, revoke compromised credentials, or initiate forensic investigations, reducing the need for manual security intervention.

While blockchain-based security solutions are still in their early stages, their potential for enhancing cloud security, reducing insider threats, and decentralizing access control makes them a promising technology for the future. As businesses explore multi-cloud and edge computing architectures, decentralized security frameworks will provide greater transparency, resilience, and trust in cloud security operations.

The future of cloud security will be defined by intelligence, automation, and decentralization. Organizations that embrace AI-driven threat detection, blockchain-based security models, and proactive cybersecurity governance will gain a significant advantage in mitigating threats, ensuring compliance, and maintaining customer trust. The convergence of predictive security analytics, Zero Trust architectures, and decentralized security solutions will reshape how cloud environments are protected, monitored, and managed.

However, technology alone is not enough. Businesses must build a strong security culture, invest in continuous cybersecurity education, and prioritize ethical security practices to ensure that cloud security strategies remain effective, transparent, and resilient. The organizations that commit to security innovation, adapt to emerging threats, and foster a collaborative security mindset will lead the next generation of secure, cloud-driven enterprises.

In the years ahead, cloud security will no longer be a reactive function—it will be an autonomous, intelligent, and self-defending ecosystem. Businesses that take a proactive stance, leverage next-generation security technologies, and integrate human expertise into security decision-making will not only protect their digital assets but also enable a safer, more resilient cloud future.

As we step into this new era of cybersecurity evolution, one truth remains constant: only the organizations that innovate, anticipate, and secure their cloud environments with unwavering commitment will thrive in the digital economy of tomorrow.

Reviews

"A must-read for IT professionals and business leaders navigating the cloud security landscape."
Chinwe Okonkwo, Cybersecurity Consultant

"Muhammed Olanrewaju has masterfully articulated the challenges and solutions in cloud security. This book is a goldmine for anyone serious about protecting cloud assets."
Olufemi Adebayo, CTO, TechSecure Nigeria

"The book goes beyond theory; it provides real-world applications and practical steps for securing cloud environments."
Fatima Hassan, Cloud Security Analyst

"I appreciate how this book breaks down complex security topics into digestible, actionable insights. Highly recommended security professionals at all levels!"
Adekunle Taiwo, Enterprise Security Manager

"With the increasing cyber threats targeting cloud infrastructure, this book couldn't have come at a better time. A well-researched and essential read for tech-driven businesses."
Grace Ojo, IT Governance Expert